VICKI COBB'S
WHY CAN I SUCK THROUGH A STRAW?

Smart Answers to STEM Questions

To the memory of
Jason Schneider

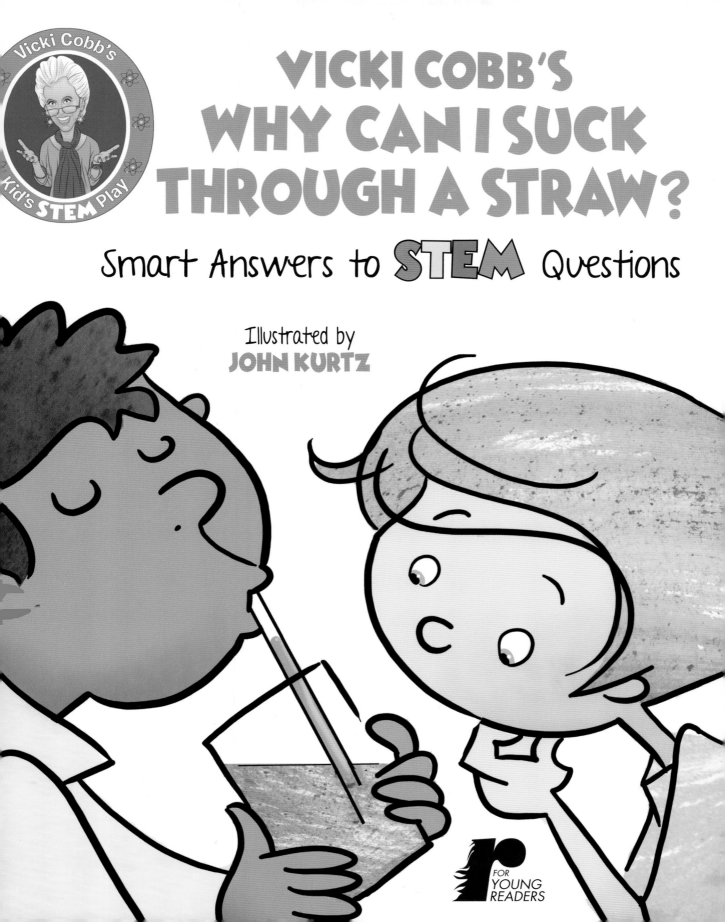

NOTE TO ADULT READERS

This book is designed so that your child makes discoveries. It is inquiry-driven. Questions keep the child engaged. Children love to give answers and very young children are not afraid to guess incorrectly. Reading picture books aloud to children is also a very special activity because you share an experience together. There is lots of room for discussion around the questions and the observations. The activities are integrated into the reading, so there will be times when you stop reading and follow the directions in the book. So take your time reading this book.

Science depends on hands-on activities and each spread is planned to advance an important concept: sucking means creating a partial vacuum in the mouth so that air pressure can push a drink up a straw. Air pressure is the weight of air and it is measured by barometers and put to use as vacuum cleaners.

Most of the activities in the book are playful and surprising tricks that are the result of air pressure. Please have on hand a bunch of 7½" drinking straws (Note: there is a movement against the use of plastic straws as a hazard to the environment. You can get paper straws or reusable straws at some party stores, or you can be responsible about disposing of plastic straws with your recyclables.), a glass of a dark-colored drink (so you can see the level through a translucent straw), a large basin or kitchen sink with a plug, a clear glass tumbler, and a vacuum cleaner.

SUCK IT UP!

Stick one end of a straw in your drink. Put the other end in your mouth.

How easy is it to suck it up?

If you blow through the straw, you make bubbles of air in your drink.

WHAT KIND OF FACE DO YOU MAKE WHEN YOU SUCK?

Make a fish face. It's the face you make when you're sucking but you don't have a straw in your mouth.

Your lips look like you're kissing and your cheeks are caving in.

How does the inside of your mouth feel? Large or small? Make sure that your tongue is up against the roof of your mouth.

Do you think there is much air in your mouth?

Put your finger in your mouth as you make a fish face. Feel what happens when your cheeks cave in.

BET YOU CAN'T SUCK A DRINK THROUGH TWO STRAWS

Put two straws in your mouth. Put one straw in your drink and let the other hang outside the glass.

Suck away through both straws at the same time!

Make sure you don't block the end of the straw that's connected to the outside.

That's cheating.

You can suck until your cheeks meet inside your mouth, but you won't bring up a drop of liquid from the glass.

Hmmmmm. . . . Why does that happen? It's a mystery that a scientist can solve. You can be that scientist.

BET YOU CAN CARRY YOUR DRINK IN A STRAW WITH AN OPEN BOTTOM

How can you carry liquid in a straw so that it doesn't fall out?

One way is to close off the bottom of the straw with tape. But then how would you get the liquid into the straw?

Trust me, there is an easier way.

Put your straw in your drink.

Cover the TOP of the straw with your pointer finger.

Keep that top tightly closed while you lift the straw out of the drink.

Surprise! The liquid stays in the straw and doesn't fall out even if there is nothing closing off the bottom opening.

Hold the straw over your drink. Lift off your finger from the top of the straw.

Where does the liquid go?

WHAT STOPS THE DRINK FROM FALLING OUT OF THE STRAW?

There is a force of nature that makes things fall.

It's called gravity. Every force has a direction.

What is the direction of gravity?

Point in that direction.

Name that direction.

DOWN

DOWN

Gravity is the force that lets you pour water from one container into another.

There is another force of nature that works against gravity and keeps the liquid in the straw with your finger closing the top.

Think.

What must be the direction of the force that keeps the drink from falling?

THE SOURCE OF THE FORCE

Here's a way to think about the mystery force that keeps the soda in the straw with your finger on top.

1. It is invisible.

2. It is touching the liquid at the bottom of the straw and holding it in the straw.

3. Its direction is UP!

4. It's everywhere. No matter where you try to hold your drink in a straw with your finger on TOP, it will work.

Can you guess what the force comes from?

Hmmmmmm . . . ?

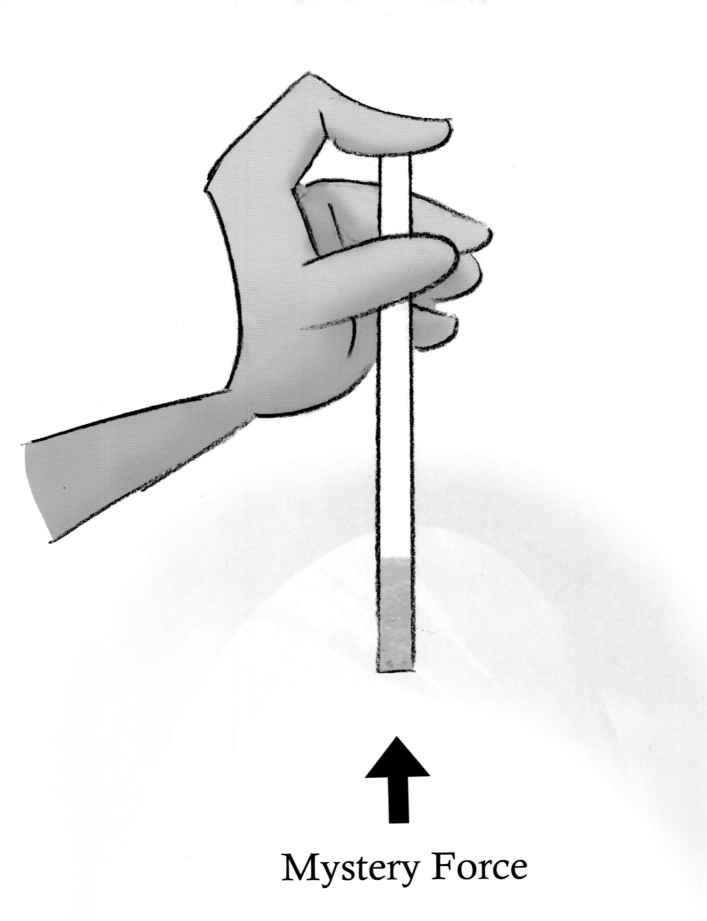

Mystery Force

OKAY, I'LL TELL YOU

The source of the force is air. Air helps you do surprising things. It's easy to forget about air, because you can't see it, and, since it's everywhere, it's easy to take for granted. You know that air is a force when wind blows. You can feel the wind and you can see what wind does to treetops and flags.

But air can also produce a force when it is NOT moving.

That's because air, like all forms of matter, has weight. It is real stuff.

We live at the bottom of an ocean of air, called the atmosphere. Gravity not only makes things fall, it also keeps the atmosphere from flying off the surface of the earth into space.

WHICH IS HEAVIER, AIR OR WATER?

Is air heavier or lighter than water?

How can you find out?

When you blew bubbles into your drink with a straw, did the bubbles go down or up?

Another example is rain, which falls down through air.

It's clear that air weighs less than water but even though it is invisible, it is still a kind of matter.

All matter weighs something.

WHERE DOES THE AIR END?

When we fly in a plane, we are six miles (9.66 kilometers) high. But we are still a long way from the top of our ocean of air.

The sky is a dark blue but it is still blue. That tells us that there is still air outside the plane.

But this air is much thinner than it is at sea level. Space begins at the end of the atmosphere.

In space, the sky is black even if the sun is shining.

TROPOSPHERE   STRATOSPHERE

1: This famous photo of Earth from space is called "The Big Blue Marble." It shows the black sky of space. You can barely see the light blue line at the top that is the atmosphere.

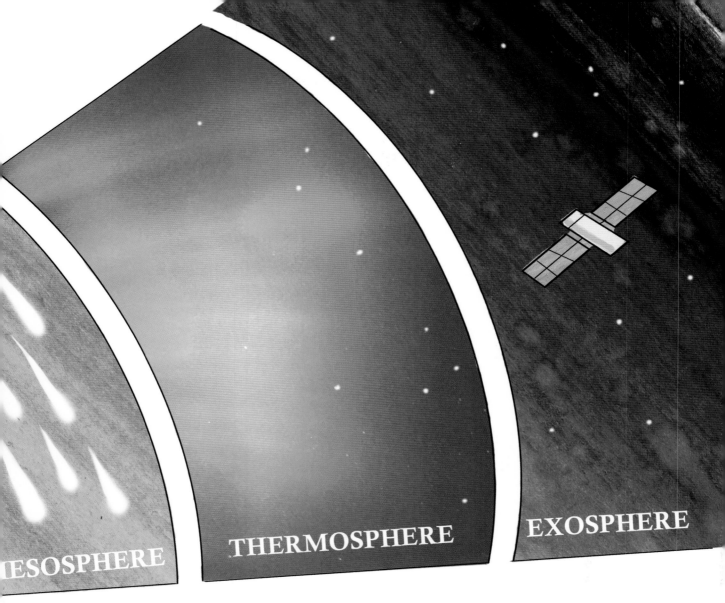

MESOSPHERE   THERMOSPHERE   EXOSPHERE

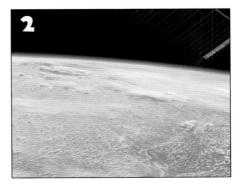

2: This is a closer photo of a part of Earth from space. Notice how thin the blue line of the atmosphere is compared to Earth. The upper right shows the vane of the satellite that took the picture. Most satellites are more than 200 miles above Earth.

HOW MUCH DOES AIR WEIGH?

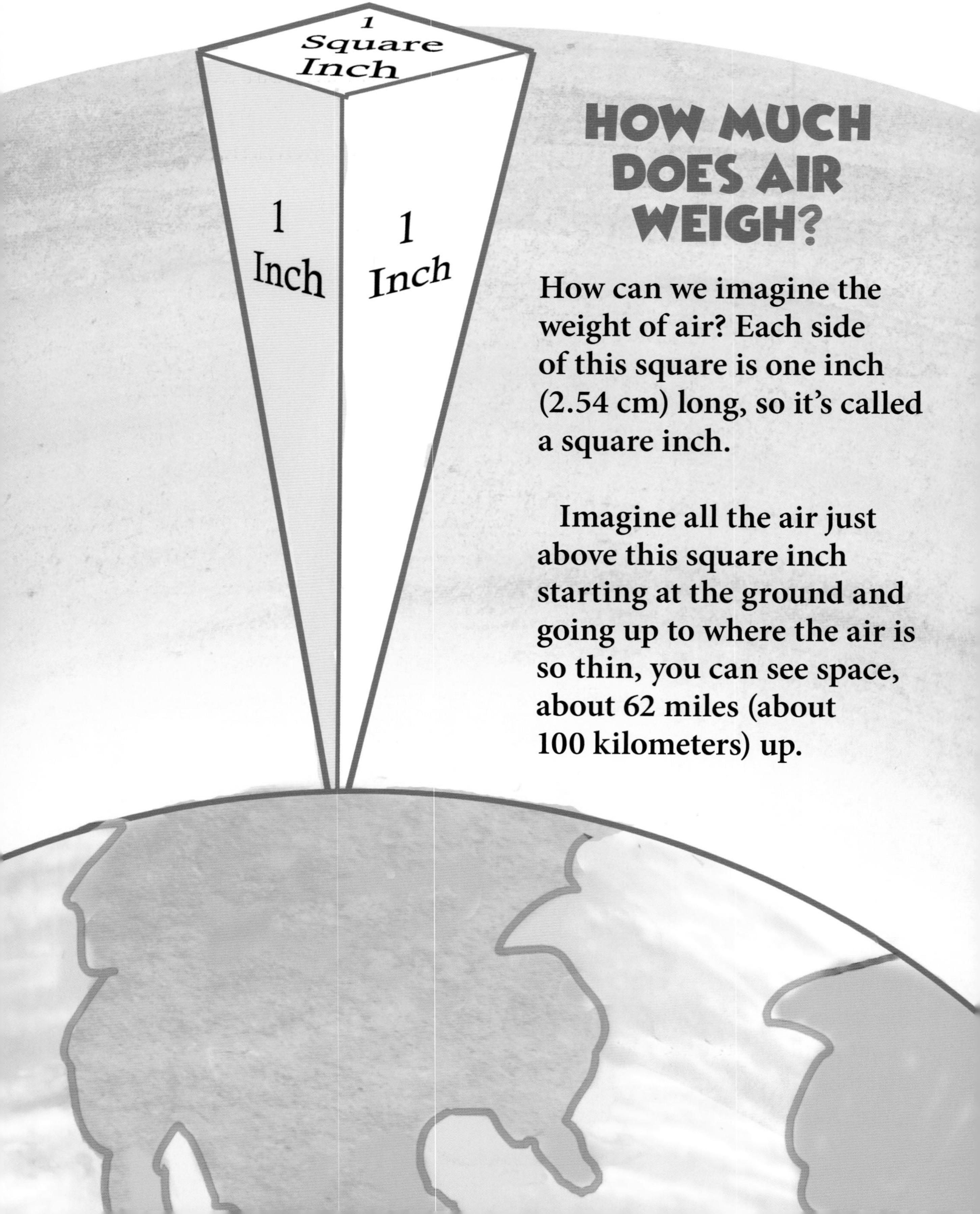

How can we imagine the weight of air? Each side of this square is one inch (2.54 cm) long, so it's called a square inch.

Imagine all the air just above this square inch starting at the ground and going up to where the air is so thin, you can see space, about 62 miles (about 100 kilometers) up.

1 Square Inch

1 Inch   1 Inch

Scientists figure that it weighs almost 15 pounds (6.8 kilograms). That's about as heavy as three 5-pound (2.26-kilogram) bags of potatoes.

Try lifting them at the supermarket. The weight of air is called air pressure because it presses down on us.

HOW COME YOU DON'T FEEL AIR PRESSURE?

Every square inch of your skin has 15 pounds (1 square centimeter has 1.03 kilograms) of air pressing on it.

If you weigh 50 pounds (22.6 kilograms), you have two tons (1,814 kilograms) of air squeezing your body.

That's as heavy as an elephant.

The reason you don't feel it is because the inside of your body pushes out exactly the same amount of air pressure as the air pushes on you.

When you go up in an airplane or a fast elevator or drive down a mountain quickly you can feel the change in air pressure in your ears.

Sometimes they feel clogged and then they pop.

WHAT'S REALLY HAPPENING WHEN YOU SUCK THROUGH A STRAW?

When you stick a straw into your drink, before you put your mouth on it, air pressure on the surface of your drink is the same as the surface of the drink in the straw.

How can you tell?

The level of the drink is the same both inside and outside the straw.

Partial Vacuum

When you suck on the straw, you lower the air pressure in your mouth and the air pressure on the surface of the liquid inside the straw.

Outside air pressure on the surface of the liquid in the cup PUSHES down on the drink, forcing the drink up the straw into your mouth.

When you sucked through two straws, with one hanging outside the drink, you had a leak in your mouth. So you couldn't create a low enough pressure for the outside air pressure to do its job and push the drink into your mouth.

BET YOU CAN MAKE A WATER TOWER INSIDE A GLASS ABOVE THE SURFACE OF THE WATER

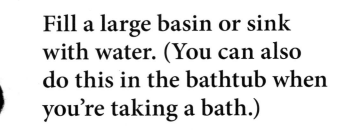

Fill a large basin or sink with water. (You can also do this in the bathtub when you're taking a bath.)

Put a clear glass underwater so that it completely fills up.

Turn it upside-down while it is underwater.

Slowly bring the bottom up above the surface until just the rim of the glass is underwater.

You have made a column of water inside the glass that is well above the surface of the water.

Lift the glass so that you break the seal between the water and the rim of the glass. Whoosh, all the water falls out.

EXPLAINING THE WATER TOWER

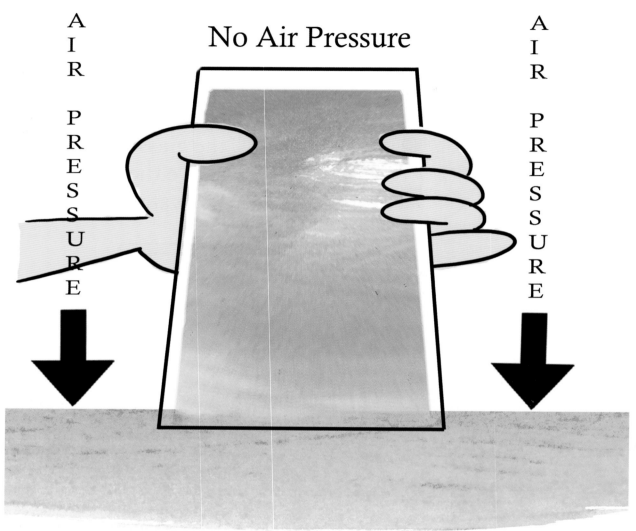

No Air Pressure

AIR PRESSURE

AIR PRESSURE

When you make the water tower, the bottom of the glass stops the air from pressing on the water inside the glass. Air can press only where it touches.

It can press on the surface of the liquid in the sink. This pressure is strong enough to hold the water upside-down in the glass, above the surface of the water in the sink . . .

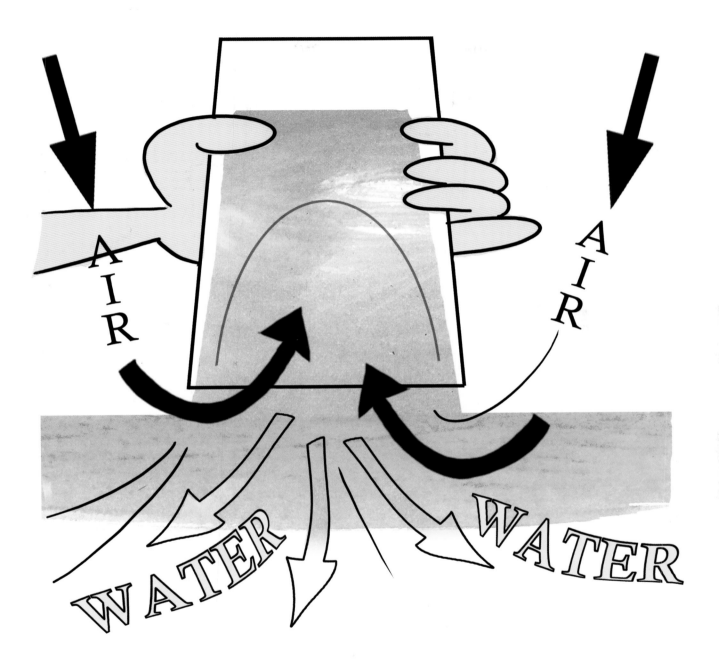

. . . until you break the seal and let air in so the water falls back into the sink.

THE DISCOVERY OF THE SEA OF AIR

CLOSED END

OPEN END

The first person to say that we lived at the bottom of a sea of air and that air put pressure on us and everything around us was an Italian named Evangelista Torricelli. He lived in Italy more than 350 years ago.

Torricelli made a tube of glass that was about 34 inches (0.86 meter) long. He sealed one end by melting the glass in a hot fire.

Next, he filled the tube to the very top with a liquid metal called mercury that was 13 times as heavy as water.

Then he put his finger on top of the tube to close it off, just as you closed off the top of your straw.

Finally, still keeping his finger on the open end, he turned the tube upside down and stuck the open end and his finger into a bowl of mercury. When the open end was well below the surface of mercury in the bowl, he removed his finger.

Much to his surprise, the mercury in the tube dropped to make a column that was 30 inches (76.2 cm) long. The air pressure on the mercury in the bowl was strong enough to hold up only a 30-inch column of mercury.

When the mercury fell down, it left behind a space 4 inches (about 10 centimeters) long.

33

WHAT WAS IN THE SPACE IN THE GLASS TUBE ABOVE THE MERCURY?

Torricelli's glass tube was airtight.

He made sure that no air bubbles got into the tube.

Still, the mercury in the tube dropped four inches.

What was in that space?

Did you say, "Nothing?"

If so, you are right. There is a name for a space that has nothing in it.

It's called a vacuum.

It was the first vacuum ever made.

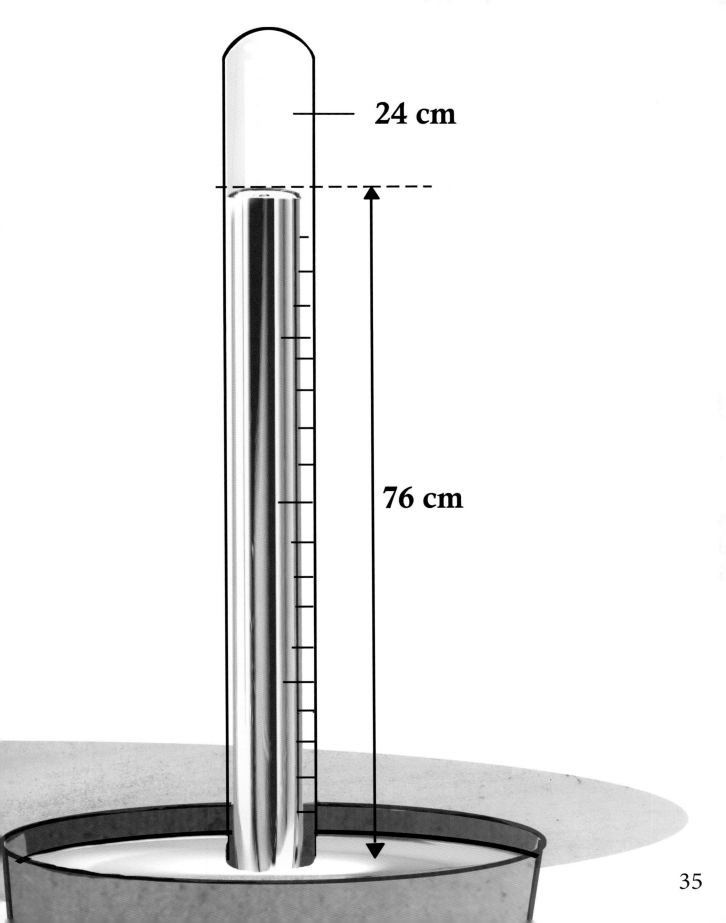

24 cm

76 cm

WHAT HAPPENED TO TORRICELLI'S DISCOVERY?

Torricelli's tube measured the pressure of the atmosphere. Now we call those instruments barometers. This barometer measures air pressure in centimeters of mercury.

Changes in the weather show up on barometers. When it is raining, air pressure is lower than it is on a bright, clear, sunny day. Today there are many different kinds of barometers.

They are important measuring tools for the meteorologists who predict the weather.

VACUUM PUMPS

Torricelli's vacuum may have been the first vacuum ever created on Earth, but it was not the last. Many inventors got to work making pumps that could remove air from a closed space. About one hundred years ago, several people got the idea of a vacuum cleaner.

Do you have one in your house?

FAN MOTOR

Turn it on and feel the power of the suction where it cleans your floor.

The air that was pumped out to create the partial vacuum so that air pressure could push the dirt up into a bag comes out someplace else on your machine.

Can you find the exhaust wind?

Feel around for it.

WHERE ARE THE SCIENCE, TECHNOLOGY, ENGINEERING, AND MATH?

You are a scientist when you experiment with your straw and learn about air pressure. Torricelli was a scientist who measured the strength of air pressure with his mercury barometer. The math is in the number of inches or centimeters of the mercury in his barometer. Engineers have invented many different kinds of barometers. Other engineers invented vacuum cleaners so that air pressure can help clean your house. STEM ideas work with each other. They change the ways we understand our world and live in it.

HERE'S A BONUS EXPERIMENT THAT REQUIRES ADULT HELP

How strong are your child's lungs? This is measured by having your child suck a dark-colored drink through straws of increasing length. It is dependent on creating airtight joints between straws, which is a craft activity that may be beyond the ability of a four-year-old.

You can lengthen the straw as you go with one child, or you can prepare straws of incremental lengths ahead of time if you're doing this with a group of kids. If you do this with a group, you can turn the straw upside-down so two children each have a clean end to suck from. Otherwise, you'll be making a LOT of straws with joints.

The first straw is a two-straw straw. Make two half-inch slits, across from each other, on the ends of two straws. Line up the slits and push them together so the cut ends overlap. The joint should feel quite sturdy. To keep the straws together and make certain that the joint is airtight, wrap some tape around the connection. You should also measure the lengths of each multiple straw since the standard drinking straw is less than a foot long.

REFERENCE
https://www.scientific american.com/ article/a-really-long-straw/

Test each straw to see if the child can get a swallow. If the child gets one, add another straw. Keep adding straws until you reach your limit. My last straw was six, but kids seem to have stronger lungs. There will come a time when a child will have to stand on a chair or footstool. Make sure the straw is vertical so that you are working against gravity.

There is a limit to the height water can rise in a tube (just like there is with mercury). If there were a perfect vacuum above a column of water, that column would be thirty feet or three stories high! However, the human mouth is not a great vacuum pump. In order to suck liquid through a three-foot straw, you must lower the atmospheric pressure in your mouth by one tenth. A six-foot straw means you've lowered the pressure to about 12 pounds per square inch, 4/5 atmospheric pressure, which is close the maximum pressure reduction the human mouth and lungs can make.

You can also buy air tubing from pet stores for aquariums. It comes in an 8-foot and 25-foot (two stories!) lengths. It is important to straighten out the coils of the tubing so that you are sucking in a perfectly vertical position against gravity. The idea of the experiment is to see if you can get a drink with one long suck. However, the longest tube makes this impossible. Some kids can do the 8' tube.

You will need a ladder for the 8-foot tube and a stairwell for the 25-foot straw. Both will need teams. The drink and straw will have to be held steady on the floor and someone may want to mark how high the sucker can move the liquid with one suck. Most kids figure out that they can hold the results of the first suck in place by putting a finger across the top of the tube while they catch their breath. This way the liquid can't drop back to ground zero.

The atmosphere can support a column of water almost 34 feet (10.3 meters) high.

STEM WORDS
GLOSSARY

AIR PRESSURE: the weight of air on the surface of the earth

AIR: an invisible mixture of gases, mostly oxygen and nitrogen, that coats the entire surface of Earth

ATMOSPHERE: all the air surrounding our planet

BAROMETER: an instrument that measures air pressure in centimeters or inches of a column of mercury under a vacuum

BUBBLE: a ball-like pocket of air in a liquid or contained in a very thin film that is mostly liquid

CENTIMETER: a very small distance in the metric system that is slightly shorter than half an inch

EXOSPHERE: the highest layer of the Earth's atmosphere, where there is almost no air at all. It is more than 300 miles up.

FORCE: anything that can make matter (real stuff) move

GRAVITY: the force that makes things fall down close to earth, but that also works in space to keep the moon and man-made satellites in orbit around the earth.

INCH: is about the length of the first joint of a grown-up's thumb. It is in the English system for measuring distance.

INVISIBLE: not seen by human eyes

KILOGRAM: Another way of measuring weight. It is equal to a little more than two pounds. It is part of the metric system of measurement, used by scientists and many countries in the world.

MESOSPHERE: the third layer of the atmosphere. It protects you from some of the dangerous rays of the sun— the ultraviolet rays, which are why you need to wear sun screen at the beach.

PARTIAL VACUUM: a space with less air than air pressure. Vacuum pumps remove air to create partial vaccums.

POUND: One way of measuring weight in the United States. In ancient times it was called "libra," so "lb." stands for pound. It is part of the English system of measuring.

RAIN: water that falls to Earth from the clouds in the sky

SATELLITE: a body (like the moon) or a manmade object that moves in a circular path (called an orbit) around Earth

STRATOSPHERE: the second-closest layer of the atmosphere. Here the air is smooth and jets fly in it.

THERMOSPHERE: the layer of Earth's atmosphere where the air is so thin that it gets hotter as you move towards the sun.

TROPOSPHERE: the layer of the atmosphere that is closest to earth. It contains the weather.

VACUUM CLEANER: a machine that uses a fan to create a partial vacuum that can suck up dirt

VACUUM PUMPS: machines that remove air from enclosed spaces

VACUUM: an area that contains no matter whatsoever. Space is a vacuum.

WEATHER: changes in the atmosphere that happen in the troposphere. These include air temperature, pressure, wind speed, clouds, rain, snow, sleet and more.

WEIGHT: the force of attraction to the earth for all matter near its surface, including air

MORE VICKI COBB BOOKS
FROM RACEHORSE FOR YOUNG READERS